# PEGASUS ENCYCLOPEDIA LIBRARY

# Chemistry
# STATES OF MATTER

Edited by: Anil Kumar Tomar & Pallabi B. Tomar
Managing editor: Tapasi De
Designed by: Vijesh Chahal, Anil Kumar and Rohit Kumar
Illustrated by: Suman S. Roy, Tanoy Choudhury
Colouring done by: Vinay Kumar, Sonu, Kiran Kumari & Pradeep Kumar

# CONTENTS

What is matter? ................................................................. 3

Atomic structure ............................................................... 4

States of matter ................................................................. 5

Gases .................................................................................. 8

Solids ................................................................................ 16

Crystal lattice .................................................................. 19

Liquids ............................................................................. 24

Solutions .......................................................................... 26

Test Your Memory .......................................................... 31

Index ................................................................................ 32

# What is matter?

Everything around us is matter. As we look at our surrounding, we see a large variety of objects with different shapes, sizes and textures. The air, food, stones, clouds, stars, plants and animals, water or a particle of sand— everything is matter. We can also see as we look around that all of the objects occupy space and have mass. So, in science, matter is defined as anything which has 'Mass' and occupies 'Space'.

## Important properties of matter

There are four most important properties of matter:

**Mass:** Mass is the amount of matter in an object. It always remains constant irrespective of its location or height. Its amount can change only when the matter is taken out of the object or added into it.

**Volume:** It is another important property of matter and is defined as the space which an object occupies. It varies with pressure and temperature.

**Density:** Density is a measure of how much mass is contained in a given unit volume. It is commonly defined as mass per unit volume. In simple words, if mass is measured by how much 'stuff' there is in an object, density is measured as how tightly that 'stuff' is packed together.

**Weight:** It is the measure of the heaviness of an object. In scientific terms, it is defined as the force with which a body is attracted to Earth or another celestial body. It is equal to the product of the object's mass and the acceleration of gravity.

# Atomic structure

All matter is made up of extremely small particles called atoms. All atoms of a given element are identical in size, mass, and other properties. Atoms of different elements differ in size, mass, and other properties. The atoms, in turn, consist of three major subatomic particles—**electron, proton and neutron**. The nucleus of an atom makes up the most of an atom's mass and consists of protons and neutrons. The electrons are smaller particles and revolve around the nucleus. The protons and electrons have positive and negative charges respectively while the neutrons are electrically neutral. An atom has the same number of electrons and protons to make it electrically neutral. An extremely powerful force, called the nuclear force, holds the protons together in the nucleus as they naturally repel one another electrically.

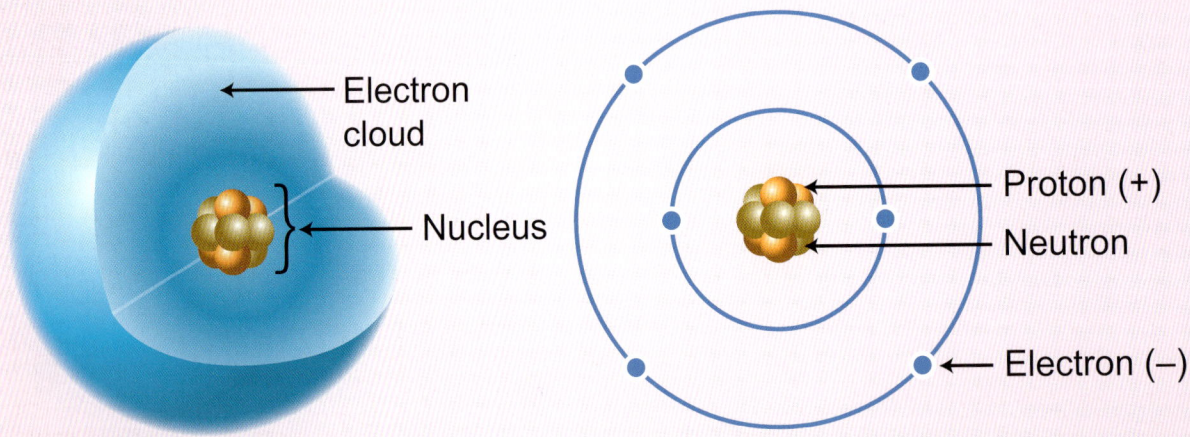

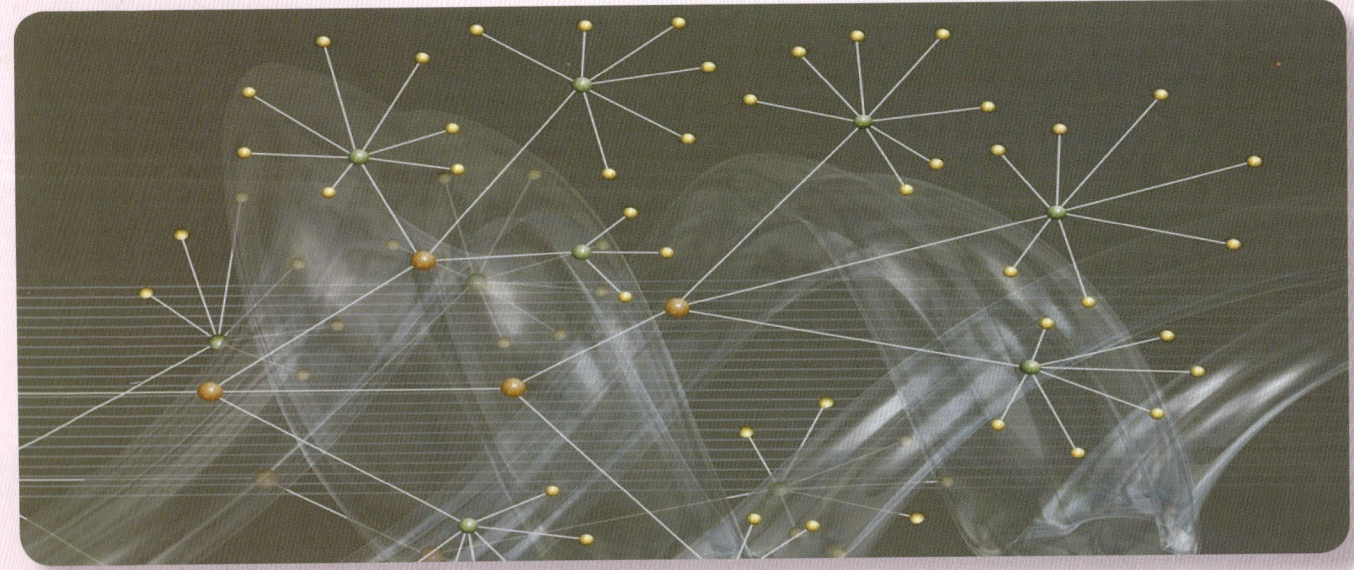

# States of matter

Matter exists in three major states— solid, liquid and gas. These states of matter arise due to the variation in the physical and chemical properties of the particles of matter.

**Solids** have a definite shape, distinct boundaries and fixed volumes. They have a tendency to maintain their shape when subjected to outside force. They break when we apply high force and pressure on them but they generally do not change their shape. So, they are also referred to as rigid.

**Liquids** have no fixed shape but their volumes are fixed. They take up the shape of the container in which they are kept. The liquids have property of flowing and changing shape. So, they are not rigid as solids and are referred as fluid. We know that all living creatures need to breathe for survival. The aquatic animals can breathe under water due to the presence of dissolved oxygen in water. So, we can understand that solids, liquids and gases can diffuse into liquids. The rate of diffusion of liquids is much higher than that of solids. This can be explained by the fact that in the liquid state, particles move freely and have greater space between each other as compared to particles in the solid state.

# STATES OF MATTER

A gas has no definite volume or shape and fills in whatever volume is available to it. This property of diffusion implies that the molecular units of a gas are in rapid and random motion. Due to this random movement, the particles hit each other and also the walls of the container. The pressure exerted by the gas is because of this force exerted by gas particles per unit area on the walls of the container. The gases have low densities which imply that the average distance between molecules is very large. So, their motion is unobstructed by interactions between the molecules. The most important property of gases is that they all behave the same way in response to changes in temperature and pressure, expanding or contracting by predictable amounts. This is very different from the behaviour of solids and liquids. Gases are highly compressible as compared to solids and liquids. Due to its high compressibility, large volumes of a gas can be compressed into a small cylinder and transported easily.

Matter can be changed from one physical state to another. We can bring these changes usually by increasing or decreasing the physical quantities such as temperature and pressure. The important thing about a physical change is that it can be reversed. For example, if we collect the liquid water from the melted ice and cool it down again, it turns back into a solid.

# Effect of change of temperature and pressure on states of matter

The pressure and temperature determine the state of a substance, whether it will be solid, liquid or gas. The changes in temperature and pressure are responsible for the interchange of various states of matter.

1. **Change of temperature:** The temperature is one of the most important factors that have direct influence on various states of matter. If we increase the temperature of solids, the kinetic energy of its particles also increases. Due to this, the particles start vibrating with greater speed and the energy supplied by heat overcomes the forces of attraction between the particles. The particles leave their fixed positions and start moving more freely. A stage is reached when solids melt and are converted to a liquid. The temperature at which a solid melts to become a liquid at the atmospheric pressure is called its **melting point**. The melting point of a solid is an indication of the strength of the force of attraction between its particles. Similarly, if we raise the temperature of liquids, their particles start moving even faster. At a certain temperature, the particles have enough energy to break free from the forces of attraction of each other and the liquids start changing into gases. The temperature at which a liquid starts boiling is known as its boiling point. For example, when we raise the temperature of ice, it melts into water which, in turn, converts into vapour on further increasing the temperature. So, we can conclude that a state of matter can be changed into another state by changing its temperature.

2. **Change of pressure:** The gases liquefy on applying pressure and reducing temperature. High pressure is applied to directly convert a gas into solid form. For example, solid carbon dioxide ($CO_2$) is stored under high pressure. It gets converted directly to gaseous state on decreasing pressure without coming into liquid state. Due to this, solid $CO_2$ is also known as dry ice.

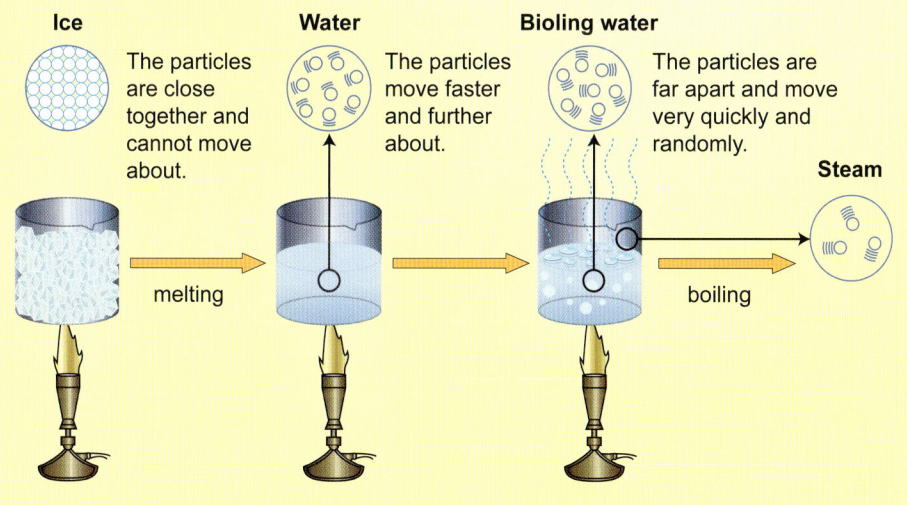

▲ Changes of state in matter

# Gases

Gases are everywhere. They are random groups of atoms. In solids, atoms and molecules are compact and close together. Liquids have atoms a little more spread out. However, the atoms in gases are really spread out and full of energy. They keep bouncing around constantly.

The most important physical characteristic of gases is that they can fill a container of any size or shape. A balloon can easily explain this feature. If we fill it with some liquid, the liquid fills its bottom part. On the other hand, if we fill the balloon with a gas, no matter what shape we make the balloon it will be evenly filled with the gas atoms. The atoms and molecules are spread equally throughout the entire balloon.

Gases hold huge amounts of energy and their molecules are spread out as much as possible. The gas molecules can be compressed with very little pressure, when compared to liquids and solids. Combinations of pressure and decreasing temperature force gases into tubes that we use everyday. The compressed air in a spray bottle or the carbon dioxide rush out of a can of soda, are common examples we experience every day. The gases escape their container, the first chance they get.

The properties such as temperature, pressure and volume together with other properties related to them (density, thermal conductivity, etc.) are known as macroscopic properties of matter.

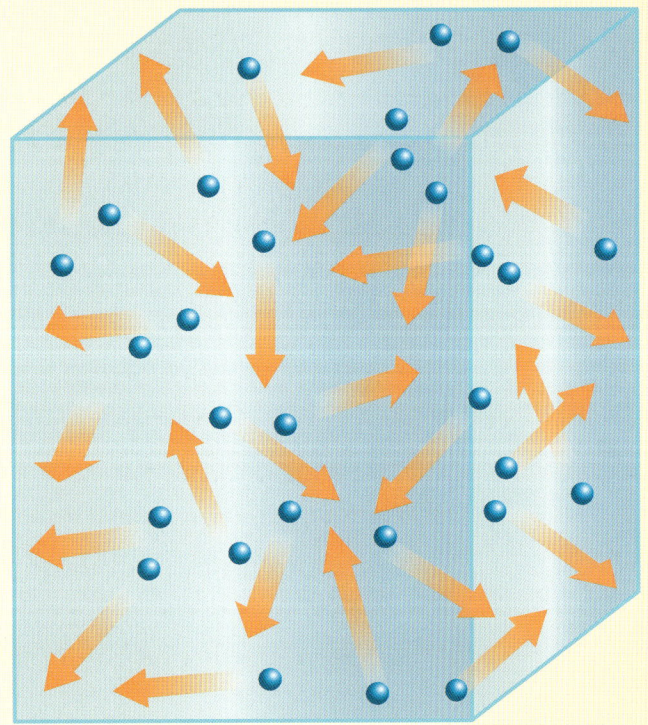

# Pressure exerted by gases

Pressure is defined as force per unit area. To visualize this, imagine some gas trapped in a cylinder having one end enclosed by a freely moving piston. In order to keep the gas in the container, a certain amount of weight (force, f) must be placed on the piston so as to exactly balance the force exerted by the gas on the bottom of the piston, and tending to push it up. The pressure of the gas is simply the quotient f =A, where A is the cross-section area of the piston.

The barometer consists of a vertical glass tube closed at the top and evacuated and open at the bottom, where it is immersed in a dish of a liquid. The atmospheric pressure acting on this liquid will force it up into the evacuated tube until the weight of the liquid column exactly balances the atmospheric pressure. If the liquid is mercury, the height supported will be about 760 cm; this height corresponds to standard atmospheric pressure.

A modification of the barometer, the

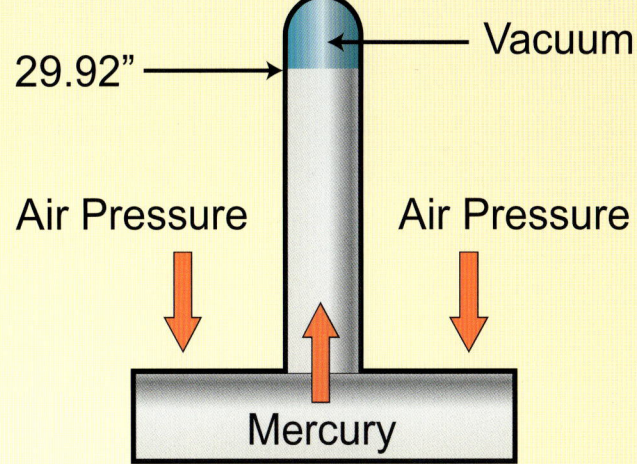

U-tube manometer, provides a simple device for measuring the pressure of any gas in a container. The U-tube is partially filled with mercury; one end is connected to container, while the other end is left open to the atmosphere. The pressure inside the container is found from the difference in height between the mercury in the two sides of the U-tube.

The unit of pressure in the SI system is the pascal (Pa). It is defined as a force of one newton per square metre ($N/m^2$). In chemistry, it is more common to express pressures in units of atmospheres or torr.

$1/10000$ Pa $= 1$ atm $= 760$ torr

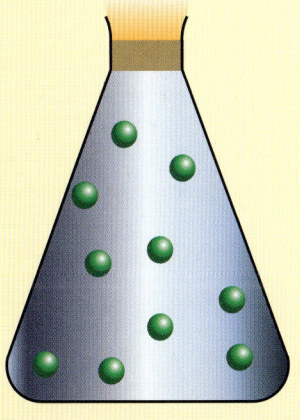

**Gas A**
Pressure = 10

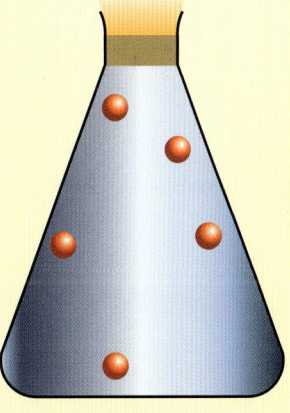

**Gas B**
Pressure = 5

**Gas A+B**
Pressure = 15

# STATES OF MATTER

## The volume occupied by a gas

The volume of a gas is simply the space in which the molecules of the gas are free to move. If we have a mixture of gases, such as air, the various gases will occupy the same volume at the same time, since they can all move about freely. The volume of a gas can be measured by trapping it above mercury in a calibrated tube known as a gas burette. The SI unit of volume is the cubic metre, but in chemistry we more commonly use the litre and the millilitre (ml). The cubic centimetre (cc) is also frequently used; it is very close to 1 ml.

## Temperature of gases

If two bodies are at different temperatures, heat will flow from the warmer to the cooler one until their temperatures are the same. This is the principle on which thermometry is based; the temperature of an object is measured indirectly by placing a calibrated device known as a thermometer in contact with it. When thermal equilibrium is obtained, the temperature of the thermometer is the same as the temperature of the object.

A thermometer makes use of some temperature-dependent quantity, such as the density of a liquid, to allow the temperature to be found indirectly through some easily measured quantity such as the length of a mercury column. The resulting scale of temperature is entirely arbitrary; it is defined by locating its zero point, and the size of the degree unit.

The Celsius temperature scale locates the zero point at the freezing temperature of water. The Celsius degree is defined as 1/100 of the difference between the freezing and boiling temperatures of water at 1 atm pressure.

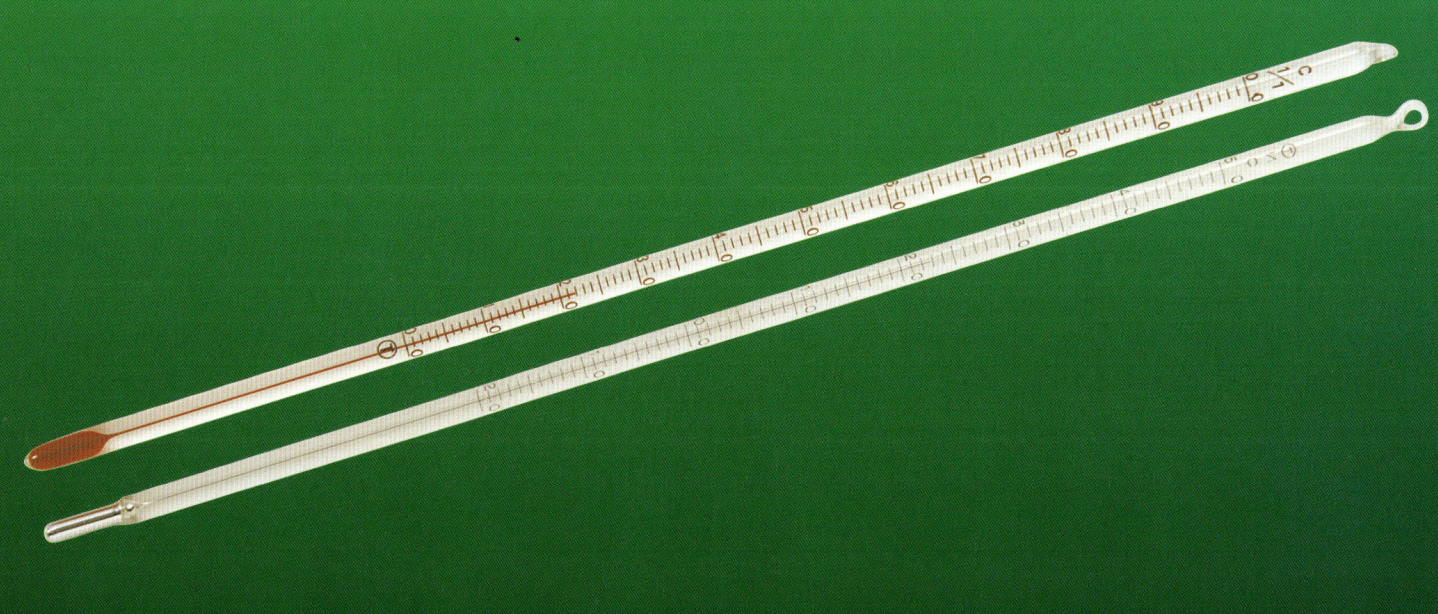

# Important laws of gases

**Boyle's Law: pressure-volume relationship:** Robert Boyle proposed pressure-volume law of gases in the year 1662. This law determines the relationship between pressure and volume of a given mass of a gas at constant temperature. According to this law, volume (V) of a gas is inversely proportional to its pressure (P) at constant temperature. Mathematically it can be expressed as,

PV = constant

At a constant temperature, if the pressure of the gas of volume V1 is changed from $P_1$ to $P_2$, then the volume of gas also changes. This change can be calculated by the following relation,

$P_1 V_1 = P_2 V_2$

Where, $V_2$ is the new volume of the gas.

So, the product of volume and pressure for a given mass of a gas at constant temperature is constant. This is an equation of inverse proportionality; any change in the pressure is exactly compensated by an opposing change in the volume. As the pressure decreases toward zero, the volume will increase without limit. Conversely, as the pressure is increased, the volume decreases, but can never reach zero.

If the graph is plotted between 'P' and '1 / V', a straight line passing through the origin is obtained. On plotting the product 'PV' along y-axis and Pressure 'P' along x-axis, a horizontal line is obtained, indicating 'PV' to be constant even if we change pressure. The P-V curve for a given gas is different at different temperatures. The higher curve corresponds to higher temperature. Boyle's law expresses the compressible nature of gas, which gives a measure of its increased density.

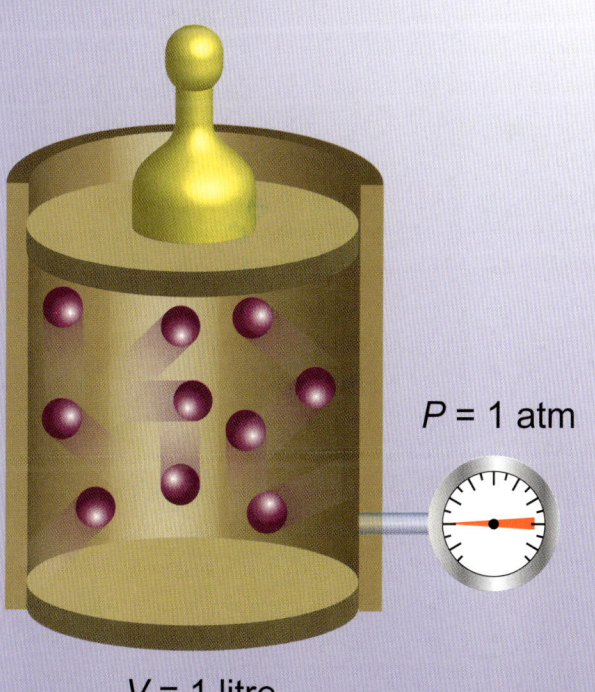

P = 1 atm

V = 1 litre

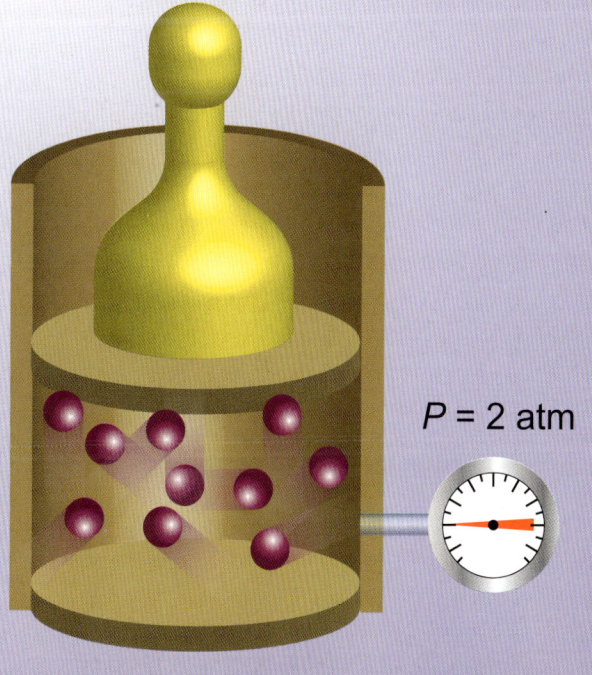

P = 2 atm

V = 0.5 litre

# STATES OF MATTER

## Charles's Law: temperature-volume relationship

The relationship between temperature and volume, at a constant number of moles and pressure, is called Charles and Gay-Lussac's Law in the honour of the two French scientists who first investigated this relationship. Charles did the original work, which was verified by Gay-Lussac. They observed that if the pressure is held constant, the volume V is directly proportional to the temperature T. Mathematically, we can write

$V \alpha T$

$V/T$ = constant

This law describes the direct relationship of temperature and volume of a gas. Assuming that pressure does not change, a doubling in absolute temperature of a gas causes a doubling of the volume of that gas. A drop of absolute temperature sees a proportional drop in volume. The volume of a gas increases by 1/273 of its volume at 0°C for every degree Celsius that the temperature raises.

To explain why this happens, let's explore temperature and volume in terms of gases. Temperature is an average of molecular motion. This means that, while all of the gas molecules are moving around their container in different directions at different speeds, they will have an average amount of energy that is the temperature of the gas. The volume of the gas is the size of its container because the molecules will move in a straight line until they impact something (another molecule or the container). However, to move as they do, the molecules require kinetic energy, which is measured by temperature.

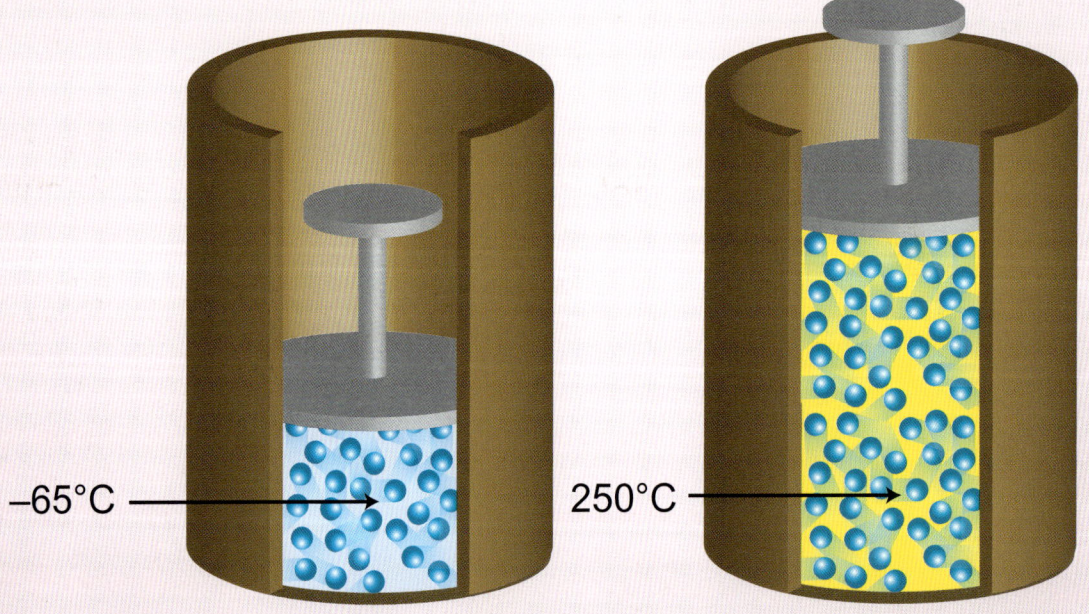

Charles's Law

So, the volume and temperature are very closely related. If the temperature was not sufficient, the molecules would not be able to overcome the weak forces of attraction among them and would not be able to fill the container.

Charles' Law must be used with the Kelvin temperature scale. This scale is an absolute temperature scale. At 0 K, there is no kinetic energy (Absolute Zero). According to Charles' Law, there would also be no volume at that temperature. This condition cannot be fulfilled because all known gases will liquefy or solidify before reaching 0 K. The Kelvin temperature scale is Celcius minus 273.15 °. Therefore, zero Kelvin would be -273.15 ° and any Celcius temperature can be converted by to Kelvin by adding 273.15 (273 is often used).

Any unit of volume will work with Charles' Law, but the most common are litres ($dm^3$) and millilitres ($cm^3$).

## Avogadro's Law

The relationship between the volume of a gas to the number of molecules at constant temperature and pressure is known as Avogadro's law. It states that equal volumes of all gases under similar conditions of temperature and pressure contain equal number of molecules. 22.4 litres of any gas at STP contains $6.023 \times 10^{23}$ number of molecules irrespective of its nature. Therefore, the volume of a gas is directly proportional to the number of molecules N.

$V \alpha N$ (at constant T and P)

The number of moles 'n' of a gas is also proportional to the number of molecules.

Number of moles, n = Number of molecules/$6.02 \times 10^{23}$

The volume of gases at constant temperature and pressure is directly proportional to their number of moles.

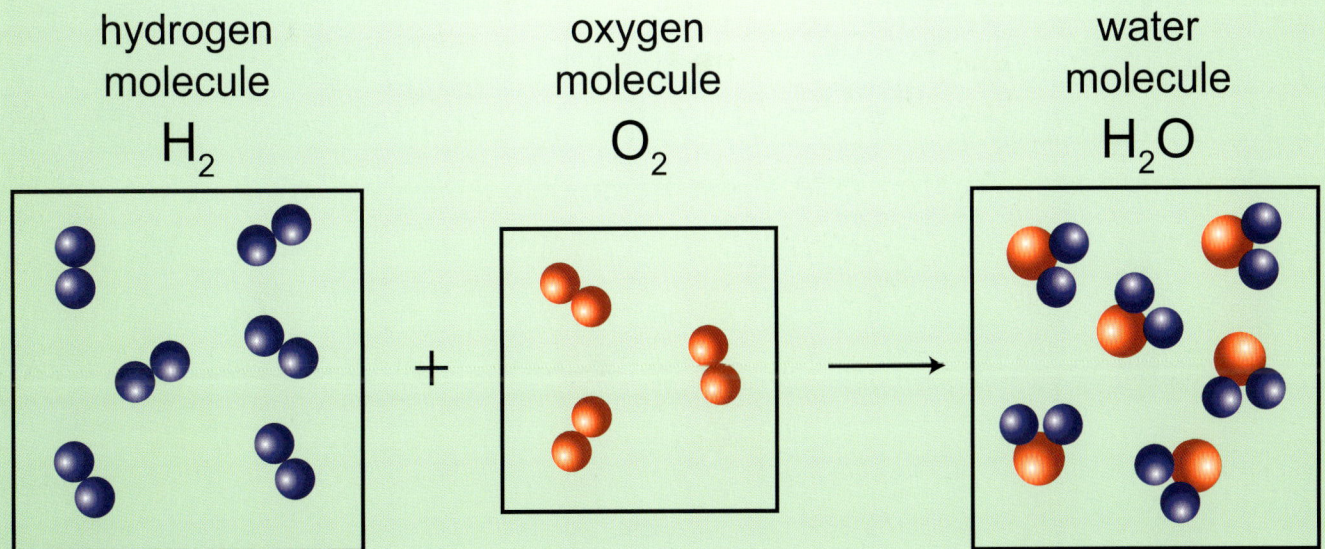

# STATES OF MATTER

## The Ideal Gas Law

The ideal gas law is the combination of three basic laws of gases— Boyle's law, Charles's law and Avogadro's law. If four variables number of moles (n), pressure (P), volume (V) and temperature (T) have known values for a gas, then it is said to be in a definite state. It means that all other physical properties of the gas are also defined. The ideal gas law defines the relationship between these state variables. This relationship can be derived by combining the expressions of all three basic laws and it is known as ideal gas equation.

Mathematically, we can write ideal gas equation as,

$PV = nRT$

Where, R is the proportionality constant known as the gas constant.

An ideal gas is one, which obeys the general gas equation of $PV = nRT$ and other gas laws at all temperatures and pressures. A real gas does not obey the general gas equation and other gas laws at all conditions of temperature and pressure.

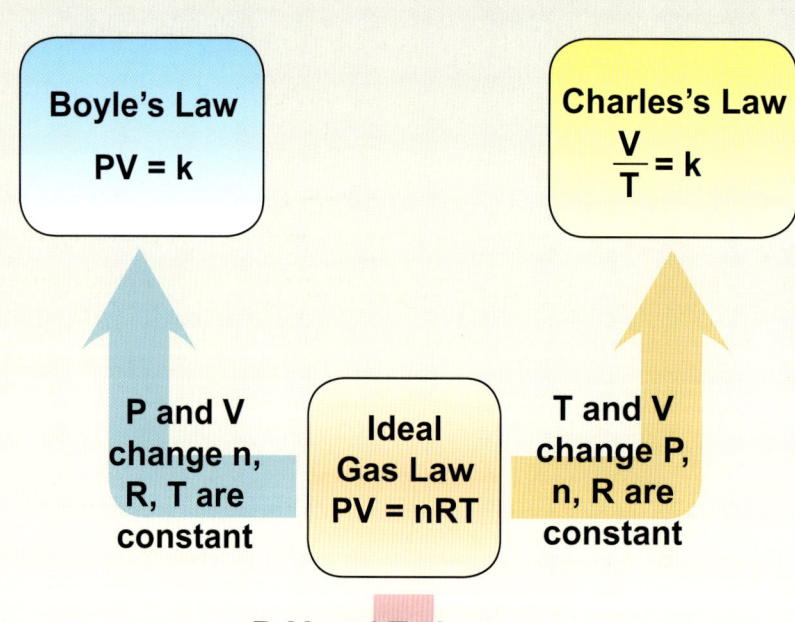

## Kinetic Molecular Theory

The properties such as temperature, pressure, and volume, together with other properties related to them (density, thermal conductivity, etc.) are known as macroscopic properties of matter; these are properties that can be observed in bulk matter, without reference to its underlying structure or molecular nature.

By the late 19$^{th}$ century the atomic theory of matter was sufficiently well accepted that scientists began to relate these macroscopic properties to the behaviour of the individual molecules, which are described by the microscopic properties of matter. The outcome of this effort was the kinetic molecular theory of gases. This theory applies strictly only to a hypothetical substance known as an ideal gas. However, it also describes the behaviour of real gases at ordinary temperatures and pressures quite accurately, and serves as an extremely useful model for treating gases under non-ideal conditions as well.

The basic tenets of the kinetic-molecular theory are as follows:

1. A gas is composed of molecules that are separated by average distances that are much greater than the sizes of the molecules themselves. The volume occupied by the molecules of the gas is negligible compared to the volume of the gas itself.

2. The molecules of an ideal gas exert no attractive forces on each other, or on the walls of the container.

3. The molecules are in constant random motion, and as material bodies, they obey Newton's laws of motion. This means that the molecules move in straight lines until they collide with each other or with the walls of the container.

4. Collisions are perfectly elastic; when two molecules collide, they change their directions and kinetic energies, but the total kinetic energy is conserved.

5. The average kinetic energy of the gas molecules is directly proportional to the absolute temperature. This implies that all molecular motion would cease if the temperature were reduced to absolute zero.

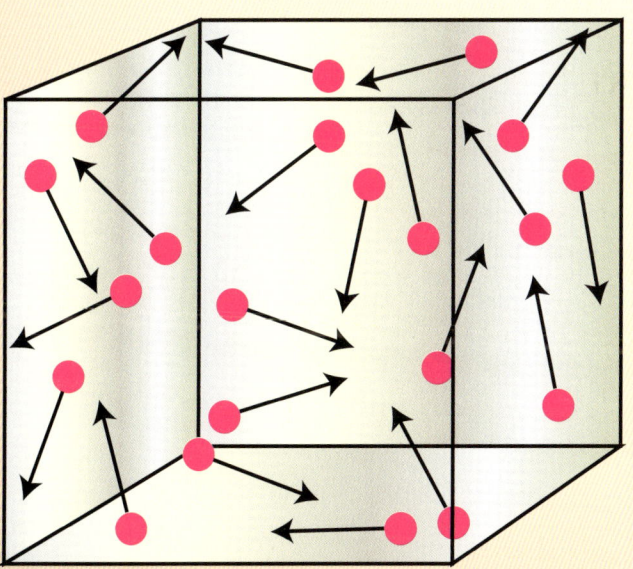

# Solids

The solid objects are rigid and retain a definite shape and volume against the pull of gravity. Strong attractive forces exist among the particles that make up solids. Due to this, particles are positioned close together in an orderly and definite arrangement in space. Their motion consists mainly of vibrating in a fixed position so their shape and the volume remain undisturbed. The atoms, ions, or molecules of solids cannot be pushed closer together. So, solids cannot be compressed like liquids and gases.

Solids exist in two main forms— crystalline and amorphous solids. The crystalline solids have simple geometric shapes, reflecting the regular spatial arrangement forms and shapes depending on the arrangement of the atoms, ions, or molecules of which they are made. This arrangement is called a lattice. Amorphous solids do not have a definite melting point or regular repeating units. An amorphous solid is a solid in which there is no long-range order of the positions of the atoms unlike those in crystalline solids. An example of an amorphous solid is window glass.

| Property | Crystalline solid | Amorphous solid |
|---|---|---|
| Shape | Definite geometrical shape | Irregular shape |
| Melting point | Sharp melting point | Gradually soften over a range of temperature |
| Cutting with sharp edged tools | Split into two plain and smooth pieces | Cut into two pieces with irregular Surfaces |
| Heat of vaporisation | Definite | Non-definite |
| Nature | True solids | Pseudo solids |

# Crystalline solids

We know that crystalline substances have a definite rigid shape. The shape and size of crystals differs depending upon the conditions under which they are grown. Crystals of a given substance are bound by plane surfaces called faces.

Crystalline solids may be classified into four types depending upon the nature of bonds present in them.

## Molecular crystalline solids

In this type of crystalline solids, the constituent particles are molecules. These molecules are held together by weak Van der Waal forces. These crystals are soft, compressible and can be distorted very easily. They have low melting and boiling points. Most of them are bad conductors of electricity and are regarded as insulators. They are volatile in nature and have low heats of vaporization and low enthalpy of fusion. For example, dry ice, wax, iodine, etc.

## Ionic crystalline solids

The ionic crystalline solids consist of positively (cations) and negatively charged ions (anions) arranged in a regular fashion throughout the crystal. These ions form a network in three dimensional spaces in such a way that cations and anions occupy alternate sites. These are held together by strong electrostatic forces. Ionic crystals are very hard and brittle. They have very high melting and boiling points. They are poor conductors of electricity. They have high heat of vaporization and so have low vapour pressure. For example: $NaCl$, $KNO_3$, $LiF$, etc.

## Covalent crystalline solids

The constituent particles of covalent crystalline solids are atoms of the same or different kind. These atoms are bonded to one another by a network of covalent bonds. These crystals are incompressible and hard. They are extremely non-volatile and have very high melting points. They are poor conductors of electricity at all temperatures.

They have high heat of vaporisation. For example, diamond, graphite, quartz, etc.

## Metallic crystalline solids

In metallic crystalline solids, the constituent particles are positive kernels. The kernels are nuclei where inner electrons are dispersed in a sea of mobile valence electrons. The forces present between the constituents are metallic bonds. These crystals maybe hard as well as soft. They are good conductors of heat and electricity. They possess metallic lustre and high reflectivity. They are highly elastic and flexible that is, they can be beaten into sheets and drawn into wires. They have moderate heat of vaporisation. The properties vary from metal to metal. For example, nickel, copper, iron, etc.

# Crystal lattice

The main characteristic of crystalline solids is a regular and repeating pattern of constituent particles. Such a regular arrangement of the constituent particles of a crystal in a three dimensional space is called crystal lattice or space lattice. There are only 14 possible three dimensional crystal lattices. These are commonly known as Bravais lattices. Each point in a lattice is called lattice point. A lattice point represents one constituent particle which maybe an atom, a molecule or an ion. Lattice points are joined together by straight lines to bring out the geometry of the lattice.

## Unit cell

If we observe the complete space lattice, it is possible to find a smallest three dimensional portion which repeats itself in different directions to generate the complete space lattice. This repeating unit is called a Unit Cell. So, unit cell is the smallest portion of a crystal lattice which can define it.

## Characteristics of a unit cell

1. It has dimensions along the three edges, a, b and c. These edges may or may not be mutually perpendicular.

2. It has three angles between the edges— $\alpha$ (between b and c), $\beta$ (between a and c) and $\gamma$ (between a and b).

So, a unit cell is characterized by the above mentioned six parameters - a, b, c, $\alpha$, $\beta$ and $\gamma$.

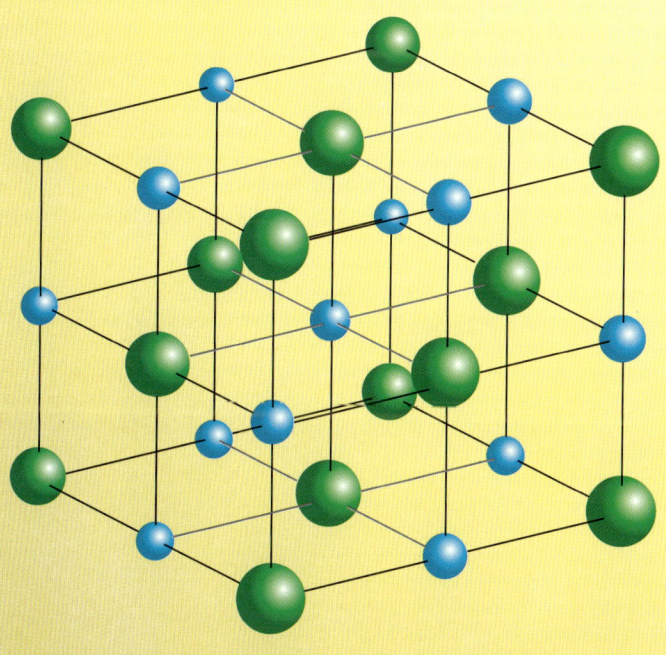

# STATES OF MATTER

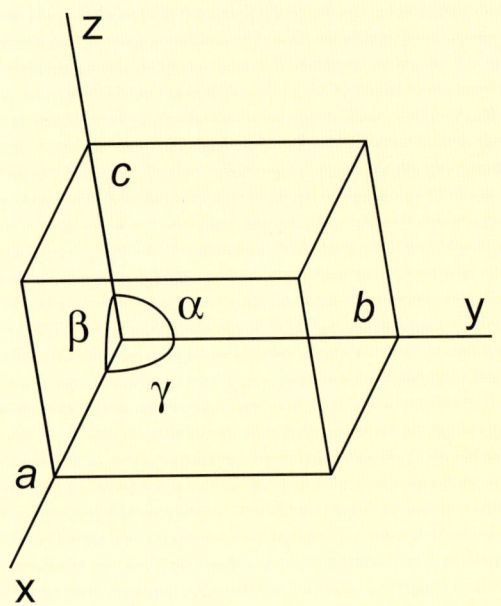

## Types of unit cells

The unit cell is determined by its lattice parameters, the length of the cell edges and the angles between them, while the positions of the atoms inside the unit cell are described by the set of atomic positions measured from a lattice point. The unit cells are broadly divided into two categories— primitive and centred unit cells.

**Primitive unit cells:** When constituent particles (atom, molecule or ion) are present only on the corner positions of a unit cell, it is called as primitive unit cell.

**Centred unit cells:** When a unit cell contains one or more constituent particles at positions other than corners in addition to those at corners, it is called a centred unit cell. Centred unit cells can further be classified into three types:

1. **Body-centred unit cells:** These types of unit cells contain one constituent particle at its body-centre in addition to the ones that are at its corners.

2. **Face-centred unit cells:** These types of unit cells contain one constituent particle at the centre of each face in addition to the ones that are at its corners.

3. **End-Centred Unit Cells:** These types of unit cells contain one constituent particle at the centre of two opposite faces in addition to the ones that are at its corners.

# Crystal lattice

## Crystal system

A crystal lattice is a three dimensional network of its constituent particles that are arranged in a symmetrical pattern. Each crystal system consists of a set of three axes in a particular geometrical arrangement. If we take into consideration, the symmetry of the axial distances (a, b and c) and angles between the edges ($\alpha$, $\beta$ and $\gamma$), the various crystals can be divided into seven systems. These are also called crystal systems. The seven crystal systems, in order of decreasing symmetry, are:

1. Isometric System
2. Hexagonal System
3. Tetragonal System
4. Trigonal System
5. Orthorhombic System
6. Monoclinic System
7. Triclinic System

## Isometric system

The isometric crystal system is commonly known as the cubic system. This system is characterized by complete symmetry. The three crystallographic axes are perpendicular to each other and equal in length. The cubic system has one lattice point on each of the cube's four corners. For example, diamond.

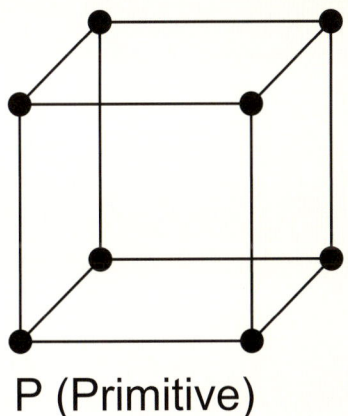
P (Primitive)

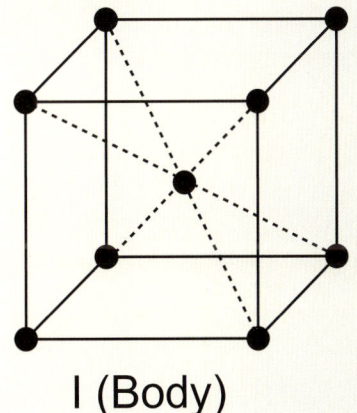
I (Body)

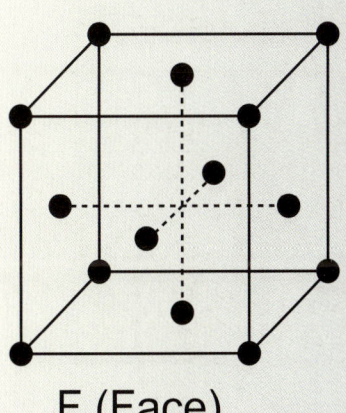
F (Face)

21

## Hexagonal

In the hexagonal system, we have an additional axis, giving the crystals six sides. Three of these are equal in length and meet at 120° to each other. The C or vertical axis is at 90° to the horizontal axes. For example, Emerald.

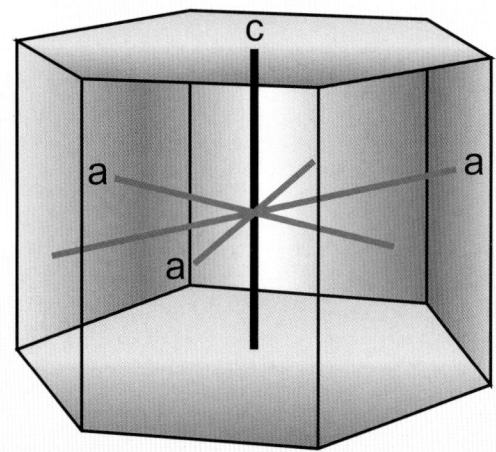

## Tetragonal

A tetragonal crystal is a simple cubic structure that is stretched along its (c) axis to form a rectangular prism. The Tetragonal crystal will have a square base and top, but a height that is taller. By continuing to stretch the 'body-centered' cubic one more Bravais lattice of the tetragonal system is constructed. For example, zircon.

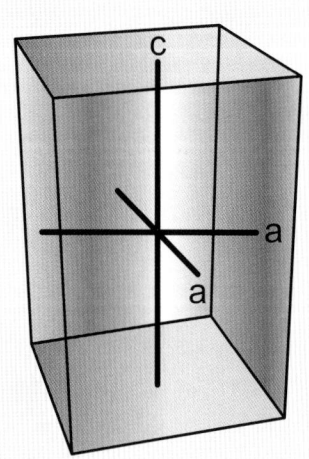

## Rhombohedral

A rhombohedron or trigonal crystal has a three-dimensional shape that is similar to a cube that has been compressed to one side. Its form is considered prismatic, as all faces are parallel to each other. The faces that are not square are called 'rhombi'. A rhombohedral crystal has six faces, 12 edges, and 8 vertices. If all of the non-obtuse internal angles of the faces are equal (flat sample, below), it can be called a trigonal trapezohedron. For example, quartz.

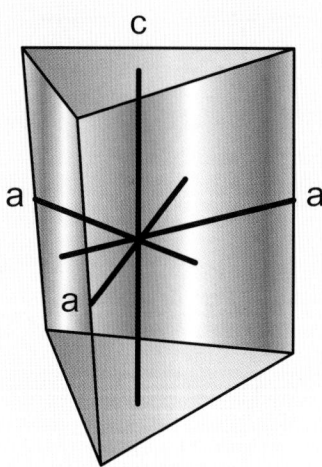

## Orthorhombic

Minerals that form in the orthorhombic crystal system have three mutually perpendicular axes, all with different or unequal lengths. For example, topaz.

# Crystal lattice

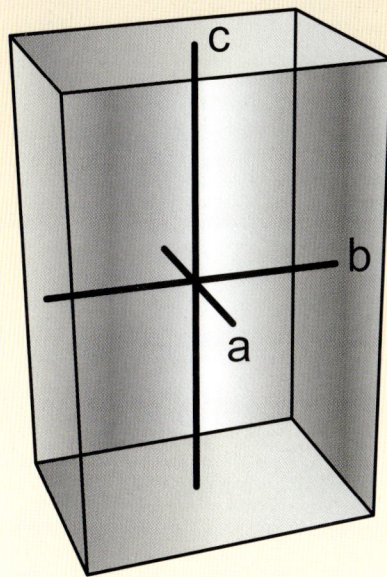

## Triclinic

Crystals that form in the Triclinic System have three unequal crystallographic axes, all of which intersect at oblique angles. Triclinic crystals have a 1-fold symmetry axis with virtually no symmetry and no mirrored planes. For example, Turquoise.

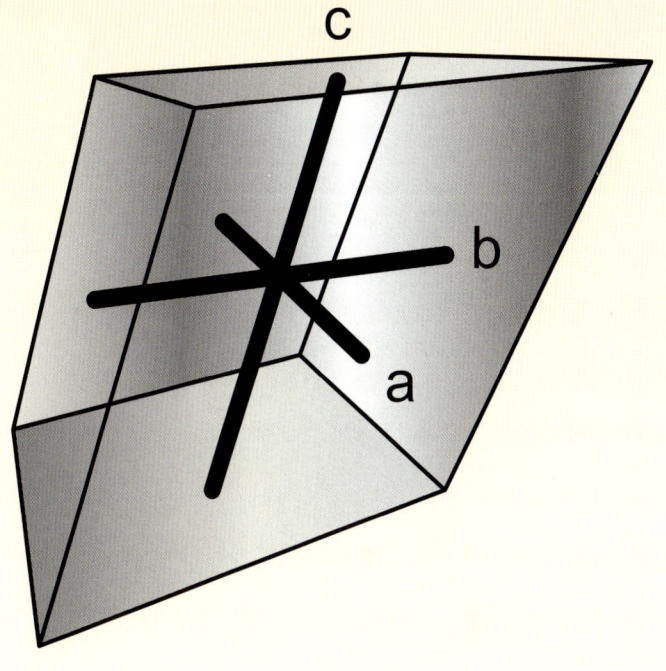

## Monoclinic

Crystals that form in the Monoclinic System have three unequal axes. The (a) and (c) crystallographic axes are inclined toward each other at an oblique angle, and the (b) axis is perpendicular to a and c. The (b) crystallographic axis is called the 'ortho' axis. For example, nephrite.

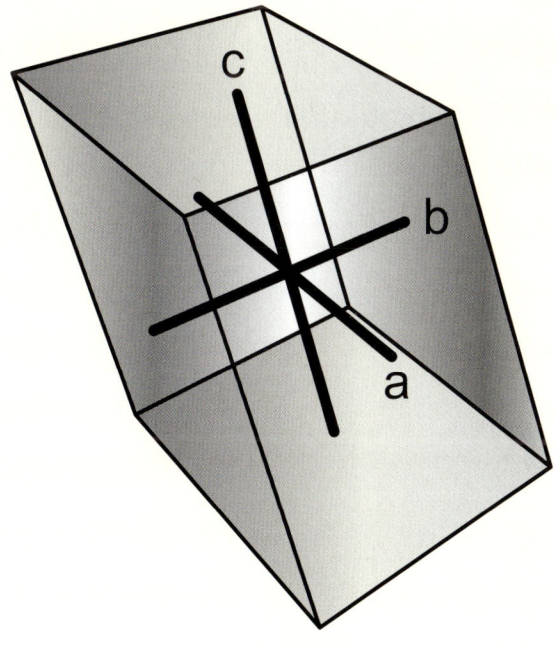

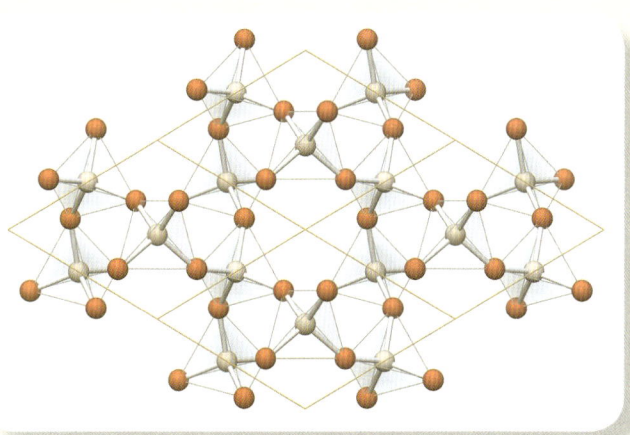

23

# Liquids

The liquid state sometimes is described simply as the state that occurs between the solid and gaseous states, and for simple molecules this distinction is unambiguous. There are much greater forces of attraction between the particles in a liquid compared to gases, but not quite as much as in solids. The most important physical properties of a liquid are:

1. The liquids have fixed volume.
2. They acquire the shape of its container.

For example, when a liquid substance is poured into a vessel, it takes the shape of the vessel, and, as long as the substance stays in the liquid state, it will remain inside the vessel. If we pour this liquid to another vessel, its volume does not

change (as long as there is no vaporization or change in temperature) but its shape changes.

We know that gases expand to fill their containers so that the volume they occupy is the same as that of the container. On the other hand, solids retain both their shape and volume when moved from one container to another. So, the above mentioned two properties are sufficient for distinguishing the liquid state from the solid and gas states.

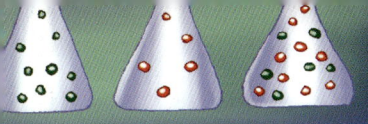

# Liquids

A liquid lacks both the strong spatial order of a solid and the absence of order of a gas that results from the low density of gases. The combination of high density and partial order in liquids creates difficulties in developing quantitatively acceptable theories of liquids. The theories of liquid state generally follow the basic theory of substances —known as Kinetic Molecular Theory. This theory states that matter consists of particles in constant motion and that this motion is the manifestation of thermal energy. The greater the thermal energy of the particle, the faster it moves.

If the molecules of a solid object are large and rigid, it may melt to an anisotropic liquid. Anisotropy is a state of matter in which the constituent particles are not uniform in all directions and the molecules are free to move. Such a state is called a **liquid crystal**. Anisotropy produces changes in the refractive index and leads to unusual optical effects. Refractive index defines the change in direction of light when it passes from one medium into another. Liquid crystals have wide industrial applications in temperature-sensing devices. They are also used in display units of watches and calculators.

Liquids maybe divided into two general categories— pure

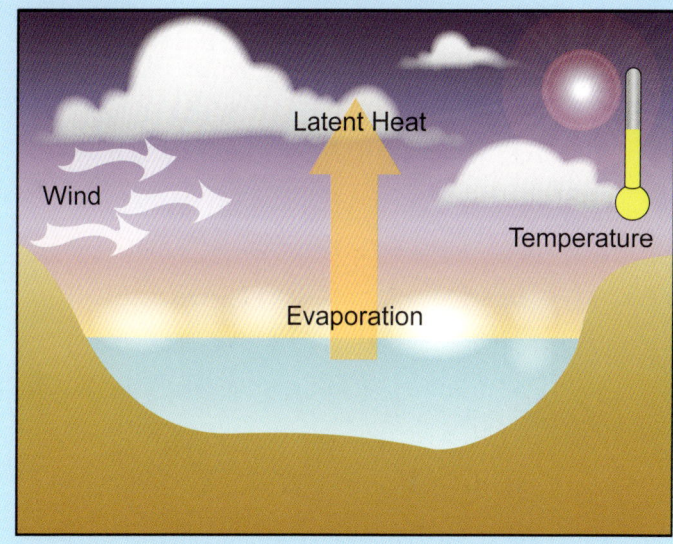

liquids and liquid mixtures. On Earth, water is the most abundant liquid, although much of the water with which organisms come into contact is not in pure form but is a mixture in which various substances are dissolved. The liquid mixtures may contain substances that in their pure form maybe liquids, solids or gases.

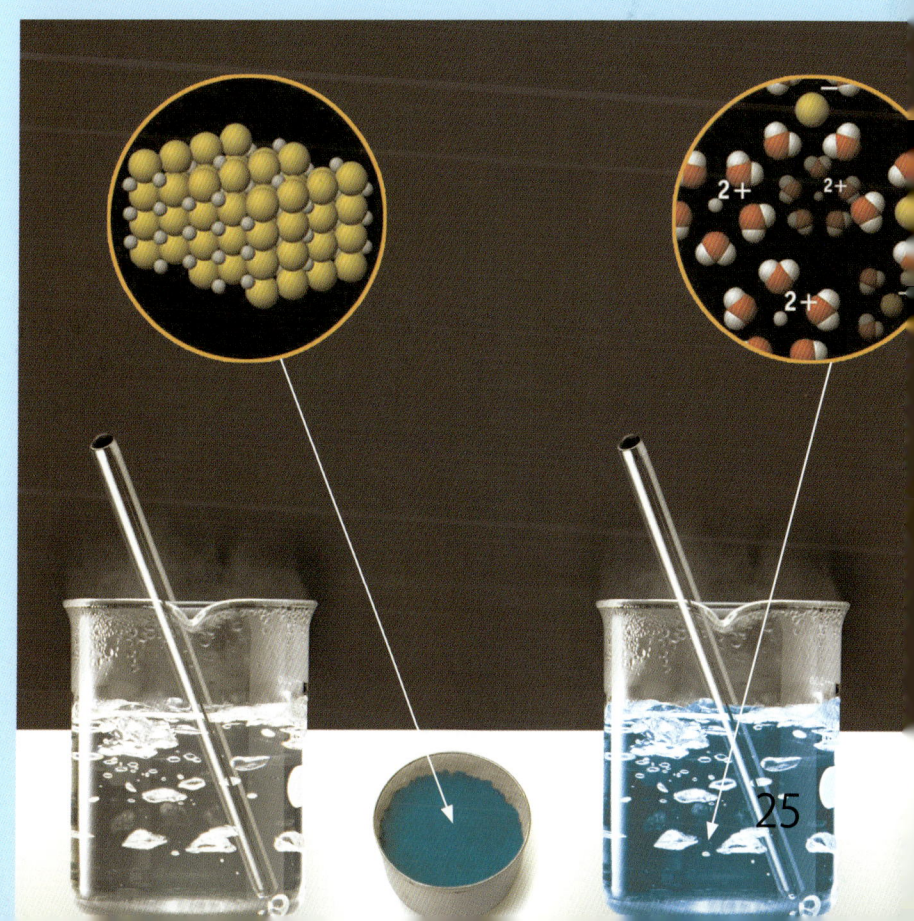

# Solutions

The ability of liquids to dissolve solids, other liquids or gases is one of the fundamental phenomena of nature. We encounter this everyday in our life. A solution is a mixture of two or more chemically distinct substances that is said to be homogeneous on the molecular scale. Although the word 'solution' is commonly applied to the liquids but solutions of solids and gases are also possible. The solutions can occur in three phases – gas, liquid and solid phases. The ability of one substance to dissolve another depends always on the chemical nature of the substances, most frequently on the temperature and pressure. The solubility of one fluid in another maybe complete or partial.

Solvent and solute after combining together, make up a solution. However, there is one condition that defines a solution; the solute should dissolve homogeneously in the solvent, only then will you get a solution. In a solution, solvent is defined as the base substance, wherein the solute is being dissolved. So, a solute is a substance that is dissolved into the solvent. It is not mandatory that a solution should be made up of only one solute and one solvent. In short, a solution can be prepared by combining two or more substances, provided the solutes are dissolving in the solvents. When a solute dissolves in a solvent, it becomes invisible. This does not mean that the solute has disappeared into the solvent. While measuring the overall mass of the solution, you can still find out the mass of the solute. The phenomenon behind a solute dissolving in a solvent is that the solute is broken down into minute invisible particles, which remain evenly distributed within the solvent molecules.

Solute + Solvent → Solution

# Composition of solutions

The composition of a liquid solution means the composition of that solution in the bulk. The composition of a solution can be expressed in a variety of ways, the simplest of which is the weight fraction or weight per cent. For example, the salt content of seawater is about 3.5 per cent, it means that there is 3.5 grams salt in 100 grams of seawater. For a fundamental understanding of solution properties, however, it is often useful to express composition in terms of molecular units such as molecular concentration, molality, or mole fraction.

## Molarity

Molecular concentration is the number of molecules of a particular component per unit volume. Since the number of molecules in a litre or even a cubic centimetre is enormous, it has become common practice to use what are called molar, rather than molecular, quantities. A mole is the gram-molecular weight of a substance and, therefore, also Avogadro's number of molecules ($6.02 \times 10^{23}$). Thus, the number of moles in a sample is the weight of the sample divided by the molecular weight of the substance. It is also the number of molecules in the sample divided by Avogadro's number. Instead of using molecular concentration, it is more convenient to use molar concentration. Concentration in moles per litre is known as molarity and is usually designated by the letter M.

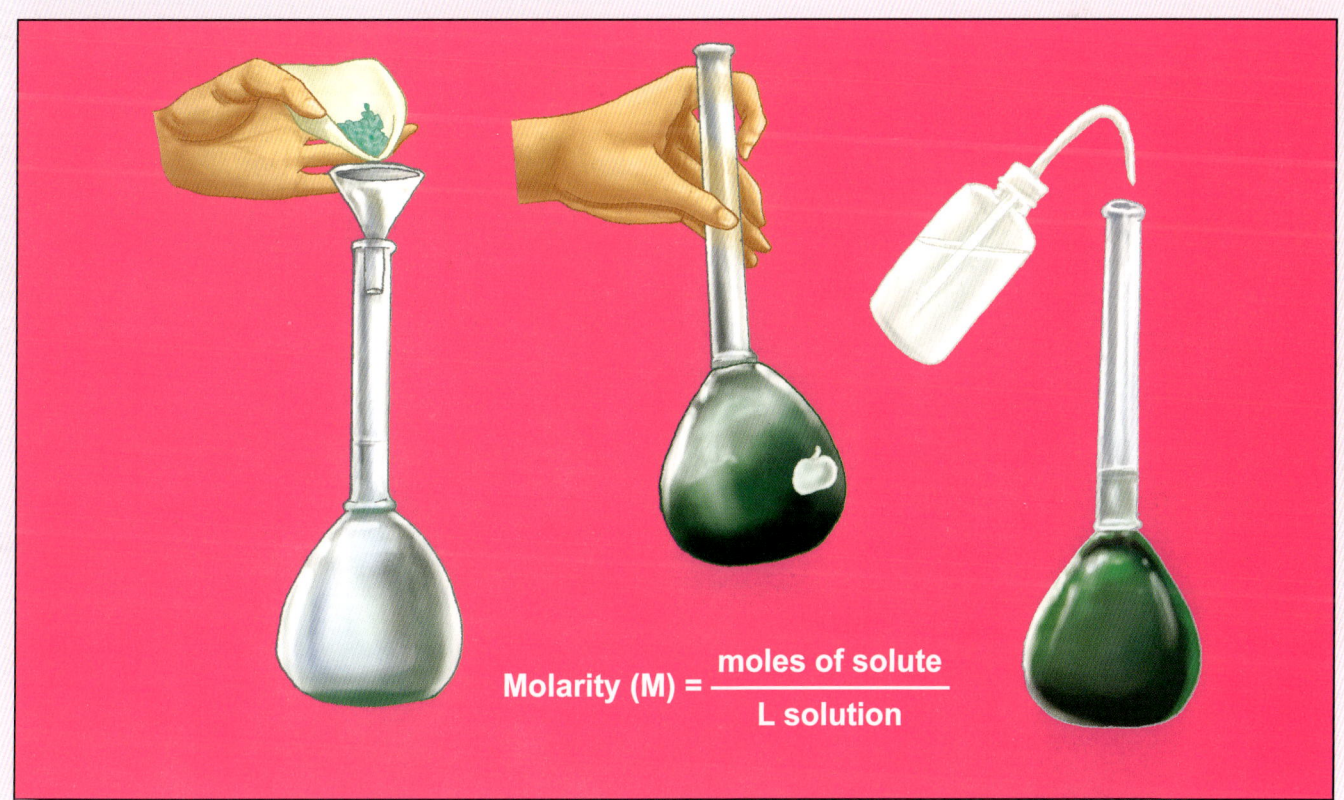

$$\text{Molarity (M)} = \frac{\text{moles of solute}}{\text{L solution}}$$

## Molality

In electrolyte solutions it is common to distinguish between the solvent (usually water) and the dissolved substance or solute which dissociates into ions. For solutions it is useful to express composition in terms of molality, designated as m. It is a unit proportional to the number of undissociated solute molecules (number of ions) per 1,000 grams of solvent. The number of molecules or ions in 1,000 grams of solvent usually is very large, so molality is defined as the number of moles per 1,000 grams of solvent.

## Mole fraction

It often is useful to express the composition of non-electrolyte solutions in terms of mole fraction or mole percentage. In a binary mixture— a mixture of two components, 1 and 2, there are two mole fractions, x and y, which satisfy the relation $x + y = 1$. The mole fraction x is the fraction of molecules of species 1 in the solution, and y is the fraction of molecules of species 2 in the solution.

## Volume fraction

The composition of a non-electrolyte solution containing very large molecules, known as polymers, is most conveniently expressed by the volume fraction. For example, the volume of polymer used to prepare the solution divided by the sum of that volume of polymer and the volume of the solvent.

## Colligative properties of solutions

Colligative properties are defined as the properties of solutions that depend on the number of molecules in a given volume of solvent and not on the properties of the molecules. So, these properties of solutions depend on the concentration of solute particles. These properties depend on the lowering of the escaping tendency of solvent particles by the addition of solute particles. The colligative properties include vapour pressure lowering, boiling-point elevation, freezing-point depression and osmotic pressure.

## Vapour pressure lowering

The escaping tendency of a solvent is measured by its vapour pressure. Vapour pressure measures the concentration of solvent molecules in the gas phase. Adding a non-volatile solute lowers the vapour pressure of the solvent since a smaller proportion of the molecules at the surface of the solution are solvent molecules, fewer solvent molecules can escape from the solution compared to the pure solvent. The quantitative relationship between vapour pressure lowering and concentration in an ideal solution is stated by Raoult's Law. This law states that for an ideal solution the partial vapour pressure of a component in solution is equal to the mole fraction of that component times its vapour pressure.

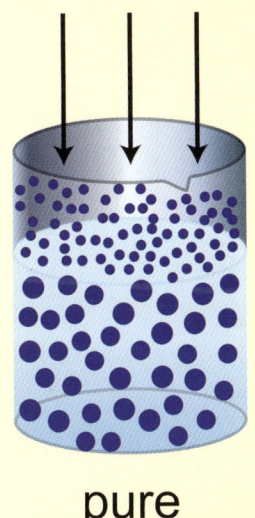

pure

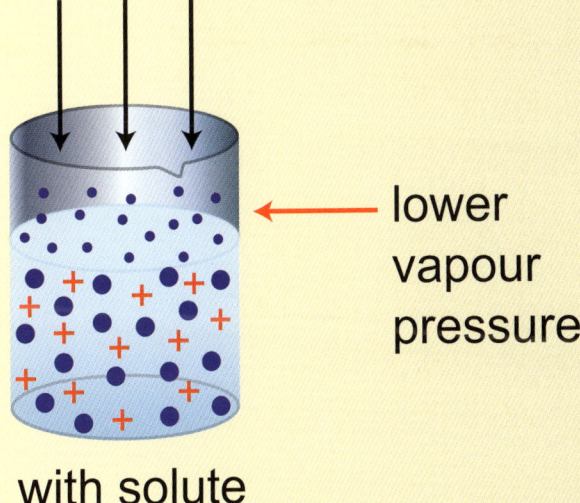

with solute

# STATES OF MATTER

## Boiling-point elevation

A liquid boils at the temperature at which its vapour pressure equals atmospheric pressure. The presence of a non-volatile solute lowers the vapour pressure of a solution, so it is necessary to heat the solution to a higher temperature in order for it to boil. The amount by which the boiling point is raised is known as the boiling point elevation.

The boiling-point elevation is proportional to the concentration of solute particles expressed as moles of solute per kilogram of solvent.

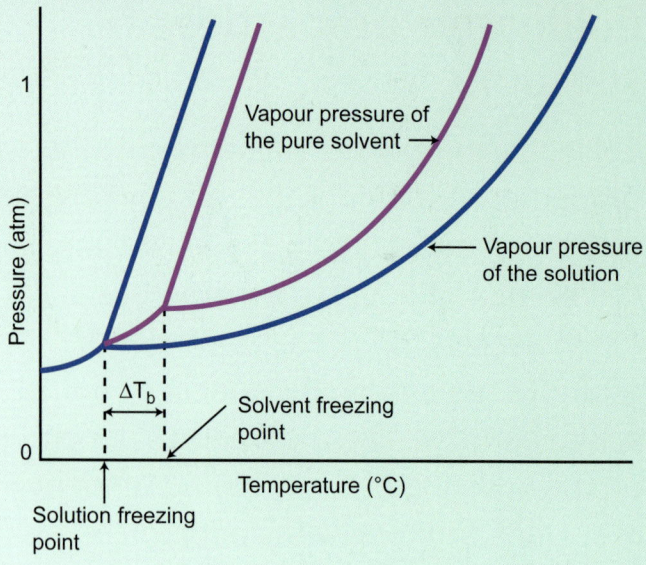

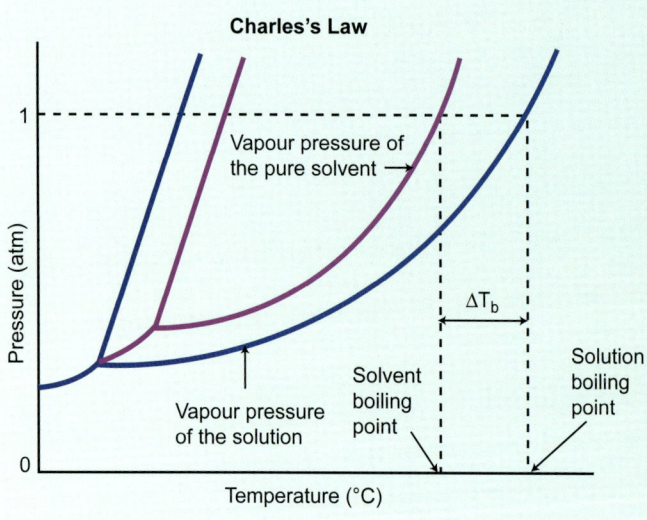

## Freezing-point depression

The presence of a non-volatile solute lowers the freezing point of a solvent. In order to freeze the solvent, it must be cooled to a lower temperature in order to compensate for its lower escaping tendency. The amount by which the freezing point is lowered is known as the freezing point depression. The freezing-point depression is proportional to the concentration of solute particles expressed as moles of solute per kilogram of solvent.

## Osmotic pressure

When two liquids, such as a solvent and a solution are separated by a semi-permeable membrane that allows only solvent molecules to pass through, then there is a net transfer of solvent molecules from the solvent to the solution. This process is called osmosis. Osmosis can be stopped by applying pressure to compensate for the difference in escaping tendencies. The pressure required to stop osmosis is called osmotic pressure. In dilute solutions, osmotic pressure is directly proportional to the molarity of the solution and its temperature in Kelvin.

# Test Your MEMORY

1. What do you understand by matter?

2. Describe the various properties of matter.

3. Name the three states of matter.

4. How can you distinguish liquids from solids and gases?

5. Define a unit cell of a crystal.

6. What is the difference between crystalline solids and amorphous solids?

7. Explain Boyle's law and Charles's law.

8. Write down the ideal gas equation.

9. Define molarity.

10. What are the colligative properties of solutions?

11. What is the effect of change of temperature on states of matter?

12. Explain the kinetic theory of gases.

# Index

## A
anisotropy  25
Atmospheric pressure  7, 9, 29, 30
Avogadro's Law  13, 14

## B
barometer  9
boiling point elevation  30
Boyle's Law  11, 14
bravais lattices  19

## C
Celsius  10, 12
Charles's Law  12, 14
collisions  15
compressibility  6
conductors of electricity  17, 18
crystal lattice  19, 21
crystalline solids  16, 17, 18, 19
crystallographic axes  21, 23

## D
density  3, 8, 10, 11, 15, 25

## E
electron  4
electrostatic forces  17

## I
isometric system  21

## K
Kelvin temperature scale  13
kinetic energy  7, 12, 13, 15
Kinetic Molecular Theory  15, 25

## L
liquids  5, 6, 7, 8, 16, 24, 25, 26, 30

## M
Mass  3
melting point  7, 16
Molarity  27

## N
neutron  4

## O
osmosis  30
osmotic pressure  29, 30

## P
perpendicular axes  22
physical state  6
pressure  3, 5, 6, 7, 8, 9, 10, 11, 12, 13, 14, 15, 17, 26, 29, 30
prism  22
proton  4

## S
SI system  9
solids  5, 6, 7, 8, 16, 17, 18, 19
solution  26, 27, 28, 29, 30
solvent  26, 28, 29, 30

## T
thermal conductivity  8, 15
thermometer  10
trigonal trapezohedron  22

## U
U-tube manometer  9

## V
vapour pressure  17, 29, 30
vertices  22
volume  3, 6, 8, 10, 11, 12, 13, 14, 15, 16, 24, 27, 28, 29

## W
weight  3, 9, 27